every day
with Jesus

365 DEVOTIONALS IN 140 CHARACTERS OR LESS

Every Day With Jesus
365 devotions in 140 characters or less
Published by Compass Media Group

For information or bulk sales:

COMPASS MEDIA GROUP
Attn: Jeremy Hardwick
2600 Hall Johnson Rd
Colleyville, TX 76034

jeremy@compassmedia.cc

International Standard Book Number:

foreword by Drew Sherman

My favorite food on the planet is Chinese food. I love it! All of it! I would eat it every day if I could. Really, I would. Truth be told, I don't eat it very often. I'll go months without eating and then when the occasion presents itself, I will devour it. It's just so great!

Now one of the things that goes along with eating Chinese Food is the all important Fortune Cookie. Best when paired with coffee, it's not really all that great. It's an afterthought. Something to do. Sometimes I read it, sometimes I don't. Most of the time the words are empty and often laughable. You just can't relate. Every once in awhile they make you smile and you kind of have that "wow" moment. But those moments are rare.

"Every Day With Jesus" is food for the soul. A special treat. Each reading takes about as long as opening a fortune cookie. But I promise you this. Every word is a treasure. Every word is timeless. And if you will promise to read one every day, you will have a lot of "wow" moments. And you will experience wisdom that will hopefully help you navigate through life's turbulent waters. It will keep you coming back day after day.

Enjoy the journey.

3

May I have the envelope please?

And the winner is…wait for it…wait for it…"Every Day With Jesus"!

Congratulations! You now hold in your hands the book with the cheesiest title ever.

Don't let that simple fact dissuade you from reading though. Sometimes a little cheese is good for the soul. My encouragement to you is to drop any repulsion you may have for the "cheesy" things in life and take this opportunity to "seize the cheese".

I honestly wanted to come up with a really cool and clever title for this book. I racked my brain trying to think of something that would grab your attention and make you think: "Man, that Bo Chancey is one creative dude. I can't wait to read what he has to say." But alas, my creative juices ran dry and I found myself right back where I started with a simple title for a simple book based on a simple concept that, when realized, has profound results.

The idea behind "Every Day With Jesus" is in every way simple. If you are a Christian, Jesus is with you always. He never leaves you. You are always in His presence. Sadly though, we often forget that the fullness of God dwells within us and we ignore God's continual presence.

When we ignore Him long enough we end up in a place where it becomes possible to spend an entire day without having any meaningful interaction with God. We don't seek Him. We don't listen to Him. We don't meditate on Him. In essence, it is like God doesn't even exist.

My friends…this should not be!

Our God is relational to the core. He created us to know Him and to be in relationship with Him. He is jealous…wanting all of our time, affection, energy, and thought. Jesus wants you to intentionally spend every day with Him.

We must refrain, however, from making this too difficult. Spending time with God does not need to be complicated. In all honesty, spending every day with Jesus is probably the easiest thing we could ever do. Jesus is already with us. All we need to do is recognize His presence and abstain from ignoring Him.

What would your life look like if you were continually aware of God's presence? How would you change if you intentionally spent the next 365 days practicing the presence of God? "Every Day With Jesus" is a challenge to do exactly that.

This book can serve as a launching pad in your quest to spend every day with Jesus. Each day's entry contains a simple statement designed to generate thought, promote discussion, enhance worship, and/or leave you to wonder at the awesomeness of God. All of the statements are short. They contain 140 characters or less…holding to the standard for the post-modern world's attention span set by a certain social networking site that shall remain nameless due to various copyright laws. Each entry also contains a passage of scripture that goes along with the thought of the day.

The instructions are simple. Start each day by asking God to make His presence obvious to you. Then take 1-2 minutes to read the thought for the day and supporting scripture. After that, simply make the most out of your day with Jesus. Meditate on the thought for the day and the scripture. Share it with others. Discuss, question, and seek deeper insight. And if you happen to be so inclined to repost the thought for the day on a certain social networking site that shall remain nameless due to various copyright laws, feel free to do so without adding "@bochancey" because that would put it over the 140 character limit.

Happy reading and make every day a great day with Jesus.

7

january

jan 1

New beginnings are what Jesus is all about. Make the most of every opportunity you have to build His Kingdom. Spend every day with Jesus.

¹⁵Be very careful, then, how you live—not as unwise but as wise, ¹⁶making the most of every opportunity, because the days are evil.

Ephesians 5:15-16

jan 2

Does your sin disgust you or is it like the comfort of reconnecting with an old friend? Jesus died for sin extermination not sin management.

¹⁰The death he died, he died to sin once for all; but the life he lives, he lives to God.

Romans 6:10

11

jan 3

Pastor is not a title to be attained, but a lifestyle to embrace. People around you are sheep w/out a shepherd. Will you be their Pastor?

34When Jesus landed and saw a large crowd, he had compassion on them, because they were like sheep without a shepherd. So he began teaching them many things.

Mark 6:34

jan 4

Look at people through God's eyes and your heart will break for this world. It is risky business to love like Jesus costing you your life.

13Then Paul answered, "Why are you weeping and breaking my heart? I am ready not only to be bound, but also to die in Jerusalem for the name of the Lord Jesus.

Acts 21:13

jan 5

Authentic worship is our response to the presence of God. It has nothing to do with our circumstances, but is driven by divine recognition.

⁹Suddenly Jesus met them. "Greetings," he said. They came to him, clasped his feet and worshiped him.

Matthew 28:9

jan 6

Your relationships reveal if you are at peace with God. Inner turmoil creates relational warfare. Inner peace births relational tranquility.

¹⁴Make every effort to live in peace with all men and to be holy; without holiness no one will see the Lord.

Hebrews 12:14

13

The greatest title one can attain is "Servant". Serving isn't merely something we do, it is who we become. Put others first and serve them.

⁴³Not so with you. Instead, whoever wants to become great among you must be your servant.

Mark 10:43

I love it when plans come together. Not that mine ever do. But I have an abiding sensation that the plans of Another are afoot. That'll do.

¹³Now listen, you who say, "Today or tomorrow we will go to this or that city, spend a year there, carry on business and make money." ¹⁴Why, you do not even know what will happen tomorrow. What is your life? You are a mist that appears for a little while and then vanishes. ¹⁵Instead, you ought to say, "If it is the Lord's will, we will live and do this or that."

James 4:13-15

jan 9

Worry is progressive in nature leading to numbness followed by paralyzing paranoia. God is in control.

³⁴Therefore do not worry about tomorrow, for tomorrow will worry about itself. Each day has enough trouble of its own.

Matthew 6:34

jan 10

Extravagant sacrifice is the purest expression of worship. What has your worship cost you? Time, money, social status, dignity, etc...

³³In the same way, any of you who does not give up everything he has cannot be my disciple.

Luke 14:33

15

jan 11

God has greatness prepared for you. You are His workmanship & He has a tremendous purpose for your life. Don't waste a second of it.

[10]For we are God's workmanship, created in Christ Jesus to do good works, which God prepared in advance for us to do.

Ephesians 2:10

jan 12

Are you running to or away from people who need Jesus? The pursuit of holiness must never prevent us from getting dirty for Jesus.

[17]On hearing this, Jesus said to them, "It is not the healthy who need a doctor, but the sick. I have not come to call the righteous, but sinners."

Mark 2:17

Pray for One. Ask God to give you One person today to share His love with.

⁴"Suppose one of you has a hundred sheep and loses one of them. Does he not leave the ninety-nine in the open country and go after the lost sheep until he finds it?"

Luke 15:4

Love for God is revealed exceedingly more through the things we do than the words we say. What will you do today to worship Him?

¹Therefore, I urge you, brothers, in view of God's mercy, to offer your bodies as living sacrifices, holy and pleasing to God—this is your spiritual act of worship.

Romans 12:1

> My favorite thing about Jesus is that He stood up for the rejected. He is an ally for lunatics, whores, the dirty, the sick, the poor & me.

44Then he turned toward the woman and said to Simon, "Do you see this woman? I came into your house. You did not give me any water for my feet, but she wet my feet with her tears and wiped them with her hair. 45You did not give me a kiss, but this woman, from the time I entered, has not stopped kissing my feet. 46You did not put oil on my head, but she has poured perfume on my feet. 47Therefore, I tell you, her many sins have been forgiven—for she loved much. But he who has been forgiven little loves little."

Luke 7:44-47

jan 16

> Christians have the fantastic privilege of getting to be light in every dark corner of the human condition. Do not hide the light of Christ.

14"You are the light of the world. A city on a hill cannot be hidden. 15Neither do people light a lamp and put it under a bowl. Instead they put it on its stand, and it gives light to everyone in the house. 16In the same way, let your light shine before men, that they may see your good deeds and praise your Father in heaven.

Matthew 5:14-16

When was the last time you got dirty for Jesus? A sparkly clean Christian is a creepy Christian. Touch the untouchable today.

¹When he came down from the mountainside, large crowds followed him. ²A man with leprosy came and knelt before him and said, "Lord, if you are willing, you can make me clean." ³Jesus reached out his hand and touched the man. "I am willing," he said. "Be clean!" Immediately he was cured of his leprosy.

Matthew 8:1-3

A lack of surrender is the #1 deterrent to fruitful living. If we believe this is "our life", we cling to it and refuse to lay it down.

²⁴For whoever wants to save his life will lose it, but whoever loses his life for me will save it.

Luke 9:24

How much $ would it take to make all your problems go away? That's your magic #. The magic # is a lie. Money will never solve our problems.

⁹People who want to get rich fall into temptation and a trap and into many foolish and harmful desires that plunge men into ruin and destruction. ¹⁰For the love of money is a root of all kinds of evil. Some people, eager for money, have wandered from the faith and pierced themselves with many griefs.

1 Timothy 6:9-10

jan 20

We all put God in a box based on the scope of our faith, understanding, & spiritual freedom. Is your box getting bigger or smaller?

¹⁷And I pray that you, being rooted and established in love, ¹⁸may have power, together with all the saints, to grasp how wide and long and high and deep is the love of Christ...

Ephesians 3:17b-18

Love is much more than an emotional response to stimulus. "I love you" is a declaration of an intentional choice.

¹⁸Dear children, let us not love with words or tongue but with actions and in truth.

1 John 3:18

If Jesus came to set the captives free, but we don't think that we are enslaved then what do we need Jesus for?

¹⁷But thanks be to God that, though you used to be slaves to sin, you wholeheartedly obeyed the form of teaching to which you were entrusted.

Romans 6:17

The American Dream is perfect for driving a capitalist economy, but is often deadly for someone who is trying to follow Jesus.

[14]The seed that fell among thorns stands for those who hear, but as they go on their way they are choked by life's worries, riches and pleasures, and they do not mature.

Luke 18:14

We spend too much time thinking about what we believe we deserve and not enough time being thankful for what we are given.

[15]One of them, when he saw he was healed, came back, praising God in a loud voice. [16]He threw himself at Jesus' feet and thanked him—and he was a Samaritan. [17]Jesus asked, "Were not all ten cleansed? Where are the other nine?"

Luke 17:15-17

jan 25

Your forgiveness can change somebody's life, but your vengeance will only ruin yours.

¹⁹Do not take revenge, my friends, but leave room for God's wrath, for it is written: "It is mine to avenge; I will repay," says the Lord.

Romans 12:19

jan 26

Merely surviving each day in vain attempts at pain avoidance robs us of the experiential joy of truly living.

²Consider it pure joy, my brothers, whenever you face trials of many kinds, ³because you know that the testing of your faith develops perseverance. ⁴Perseverance must finish its work so that you may be mature and complete, not lacking anything.

James 1:2-4

> Misplaced hope is faith's greatest enemy.

[1]Now faith is being sure of what we hope for and certain of what we do not see.

Hebrews 11:1

> Living as your own lord can carry you farther from home than you ever intended. Suddenly you awake with the shock that you are utterly lost.

[3]First of all, you must understand that in the last days scoffers will come, scoffing and following their own evil desires. [4]They will say, "Where is this 'coming' he promised? Ever since our fathers died, everything goes on as it has since the beginning of creation."

2 Peter 3:3-4

The grand frustration found at the core of the search for significance leaves most stagnated in "survival mode" as true life passes by.

29This only have I found: God made mankind upright, but men have gone in search of many schemes."

Ecclesiastes 7:29

When we refuse to create, we lose touch with the heart of God. It's better to create an original stick figure than paint the Mona Lisa by numbers.

27So God created man in his own image, in the image of God he created him; male and female he created them.

Genesis 1:27

It is impossible to orchestrate a storm-free life. The clouds gather. The rains come. What matters is the foundation you have built on.

[47]I will show you what he is like who comes to me and hears my words and puts them into practice. [48]He is like a man building a house, who dug down deep and laid the foundation on rock. When a flood came, the torrent struck that house but could not shake it, because it was well built.

Luke 6:47-48

february

27

feb 1

"Jesus is Lord." Mere cliché or the greatest truth you know? There is no middle ground.

21"Not everyone who says to me, 'Lord, Lord,' will enter the kingdom of heaven, but only he who does the will of my Father who is in heaven.

Matthew 7:21

---

feb 2

Vengeance is sickness that plagues humanity from toddlers to tyrants. It consumes the afflicted leaving no room for grace.

21Then Peter came to Jesus and asked, "Lord, how many times shall I forgive my brother when he sins against me? Up to seven times?" 22Jesus answered, "I tell you, not seven times, but seventy-seven times.

Matthew 18:21-22

29

feb 3

Godly confrontation is for the purpose of restoration, not punishment. Punishment reveals a conspiracy to cover one's own indiscretions.

¹Brothers, if someone is caught in a sin, you who are spiritual should restore him gently. But watch yourself, or you also may be tempted.

Galatians 6:1

feb 4

An advocate is one who stoops to your level so that together you can rise above the filth of fallen humanity. Jesus is your advocate.

¹⁹We have this hope as an anchor for the soul, firm and secure. It enters the inner sanctuary behind the curtain, ²⁰where Jesus, who went before us, has entered on our behalf. He has become a high priest forever, in the order of Melchizedek.

Hebrews 6:19-20

feb 5

Wisdom is a lost commodity in our capitalistic world. Unobtainable through the conventional methods of commerce it is rarely valued.

[7]Wisdom is supreme; therefore get wisdom. Though it cost all you have, get understanding.

Proverbs 4:7

---

feb 6

When leaders faithfully pray for those in their charge, overall responsiveness will increase exponentially. Pray for those you lead.

[3]I thank my God every time I remember you. [4]In all my prayers for all of you, I always pray with joy.

Philippians 1:3-4

feb 7

Today's treasure is tomorrow's trash. What are you chasing?

8What is more, I consider everything a loss compared to the surpassing greatness of knowing Christ Jesus my Lord, for whose sake I have lost all things. I consider them rubbish, that I may gain Christ.

Philippians 3:8

feb 8

Happiness is knowing what you need, where to get it, and how to use it.

6Blessed are those who hunger and thirst for righteousness, for they will be filled.

Matthew 5:6

feb 9

God is unchanging yet ever-revealing. What will God reveal to you today?

¹⁷I keep asking that the God of our Lord Jesus Christ, the glorious Father, may give you the Spirit of wisdom and revelation, so that you may know him better.

Ephesians 1:17

---

feb 10

Time is no obstacle for God. He created it. He can manipulate it as He chooses. He gives you all the time you need to do what He wants.

¹³So the sun stood still, and the moon stopped, till the nation avenged itself on its enemies, as it is written in the Book of Jashar. The sun stopped in the middle of the sky and delayed going down about a full day.

Joshua 10:13

feb 11

Misplaced expectations propel us toward false hope. What you expect reveals the security of your hope. Are you certain of what you hope for?

[5]And hope does not disappoint us, because God has poured out his love into our hearts by the Holy Spirit, whom he has given us.

Romans 5:5

---

feb 12

Great answers produce more questions. Jesus is the answer. The more I know Him the more I question. The more I question the more I know Him.

[7]"Ask and it will be given to you; seek and you will find; knock and the door will be opened to you. [8]For everyone who asks receives; he who seeks finds; and to him who knocks, the door will be opened.

Matthew 7:7-8

feb 13

It is impossible to navigate a trouble free life. Wisdom drives you headlong into the face of adversity while fools abandon ship.

[33]"I have told you these things, so that in me you may have peace. In this world you will have trouble. But take heart! I have overcome the world."

John 16:33

feb 14

The idea of falling in love lends itself to the possibility that one could fall out of love as well. God's love does not allow for that.

[4]Love is patient, love is kind. It does not envy, it does not boast, it is not proud. [5]It is not rude, it is not self-seeking, it is not easily angered, it keeps no record of wrongs. 6Love does not delight in evil but rejoices with the truth. [7]It always protects, always trusts, always hopes, always perseveres. [8]Love never fails. But where there are prophecies, they will cease; where there are tongues, they will be stilled; where there is knowledge, it will pass away.

1 Corinthians 13:4-8

35

feb 15

When grace takes root peace floods in. Peace is a byproduct of grace, because grace makes peace with God.

²Grace and peace to you from God our Father and the Lord Jesus Christ.

Philippians 1:2

feb 16

Bitterness paralyzes the soul by battening down the hatches. Love can neither penetrate nor escape the bitter heart.

³¹Get rid of all bitterness, rage and anger, brawling and slander, along with every form of malice.

Ephesians 4:31

feb 17

Sin opportunities present themselves in grand fashion, beckoning the Sinner to partake. Far subtler are the divine prospects of the Saint.

⁶An evil man is snared by his own sin, but a righteous one can sing and be glad.

Proverbs 29:6

feb 18

Worldly success is found in becoming something. Godly success is found in becoming nothing.

⁵Your attitude should be the same as that of Christ Jesus: ⁶Who, being in very nature God, did not consider equality with God something to be grasped, ⁷but made himself nothing, taking the very nature of a servant, being made in human likeness.

Philippians 2:5-7

37

feb 19

Sharing Jesus is never about winning an argument. It is simply making an introduction & expounding on what others already know to be true.

²¹For although they knew God, they neither glorified him as God nor gave thanks to him, but their thinking became futile and their foolish hearts were darkened.

Romans 1:21

feb 20

The storms of life rage all around and cannot be avoided. The storms inside blow just as hard, but "peace be still" changes everything.

³⁹He got up, rebuked the wind and said to the waves, "Quiet! Be still!" Then the wind died down and it was completely calm.

Mark 4:39

feb 21

Eternity is a reality that eludes the hopelessly time-conscious. Live today in such a way that it will last forever and eternity is yours.

[20]But store up for yourselves treasures in heaven, where moth and rust do not destroy, and where thieves do not break in and steal.

Matthew 6:20

feb 22

Evangelism is a messy affair. Those who give their lives to pain avoidance will never know the joy of getting in trouble for Jesus.

[40]His speech persuaded them. They called the apostles in and had them flogged. Then they ordered them not to speak in the name of Jesus, and let them go. [41]The apostles left the Sanhedrin, rejoicing because they had been counted worthy of suffering disgrace for the Name.

Acts 5:40-41

39

Christians are not merely consumers of God. They are participants in His divine plan of redemption.

20We are therefore Christ's ambassadors, as though God were making his appeal through us. We implore you on Christ's behalf: Be reconciled to God.

2 Corinthians 5:20

Non-thinking Christians are like 1-eyed cats jumping from tree to tree. They have no depth perception, make illogical leaps, & always fall.

5We demolish arguments and every pretension that sets itself up against the knowledge of God, and we take captive every thought to make it obedient to Christ.

2 Corinthians 10:5

feb 25

Timid Christians are a concern. Because their foundation is insecure they are unstable, shaky, & incapable of hitting the mark.

[7]For God did not give us a spirit of timidity, but a spirit of power, of love and of self-discipline.

2 Timothy 1:7

feb 26

They say the universe is infinitely large & small (no beginning & no end). Sounds like someone else we know. Does He cause you to marvel?

[8]"I am the Alpha and the Omega," says the Lord God, "who is, and who was, and who is to come, the Almighty."

Revelation 1:8

feb 27

Your life's mission is the catalyst for your actions. If you do not know your mission you are utterly lost. Decide what you are living for.

²¹For to me, to live is Christ and to die is gain.

Philippians 1:21

feb 28

Today is a day of eternal importance. It can be eternally wasted or eternally enjoyed. What you do or do not do makes the difference.

³⁴"Then the King will say to those on his right, 'Come, you who are blessed by my Father; take your inheritance, the kingdom prepared for you since the creation of the world. ³⁵For I was hungry and you gave me something to eat, I was thirsty and you gave me something to drink, I was a stranger and you invited me in, ³⁶I needed clothes and you clothed me, I was sick and you looked after me, I was in prison and you came to visit me.'

Matthew 25:34-36

march

Will you leave this world with fading memories of a life lived in vain or a legacy of faith reproduced in others? The choice is made today.

²³But the one who received the seed that fell on good soil is the man who hears the word and understands it. He produces a crop, yielding a hundred, sixty or thirty times what was sown.

Matthew 13:23

Loneliness is one of the great maladies of our time. Surrounded by the illusion of relationships the real thing often drifts by unattained.

¹⁰Be devoted to one another in brotherly love. Honor one another above yourselves.

Romans 12:10

mar 3

Life's meaning is a mystery for the directionally challenged. Orient yourself to a fixed point of reference (God) & your way becomes clear.

²Let us fix our eyes on Jesus, the author and perfecter of our faith, who for the joy set before him endured the cross, scorning its shame, and sat down at the right hand of the throne of God.

Hebrews 12:2

mar 4

Your life is not an accident. You may never measure up to the grand schemes of man, but there is divine purpose for your life.

¹¹"For I know the plans I have for you," declares the LORD, "plans to prosper you and not to harm you, plans to give you hope and a future."

Jeremiah 29:11

mar 5

A story held within can soothe the soul. A story told can change the world. Tell your story.

⁹But if I say, "I will not mention him or speak any more in his name," his word is in my heart like a fire, a fire shut up in my bones. I am weary of holding it in; indeed, I cannot.

Jeremiah 20:9

mar 6

Relationships are risky affairs that often bring grief. The isolated however will be devoured. Take the risk. We are better together.

¹²Though one may be overpowered, two can defend themselves. A cord of three strands is not quickly broken.

Ecclesiastes 4:12

47

mar 7

Faith, hope & love are empty ideals when unaccompanied by action, but when followed with bold feats the doer is thrust into the divine flow.

[3]We continually remember before our God and Father your work produced by faith, your labor prompted by love, and your endurance inspired by hope in our Lord Jesus Christ.

1 Thessalonians 1:3

mar 8

Religion is not a belief system that defines you. Pure religion is to see the unsightly, touch the untouchable, and love the unlovely.

[27]Religion that God our Father accepts as pure and faultless is this: to look after orphans and widows in their distress and to keep oneself from being polluted by the world.

James 1:27

mar 9

A vacation with God is far better than a vacation from God. He makes us lie down in green pastures. Thank you Jesus for times of rest.

²He makes me lie down in green pastures, he leads me beside quiet waters, ³he restores my soul. He guides me in paths of righteousness for his name's sake.

Psalm 23:2-3

mar 10

Worship is not an event to be written on a calendar. It is a lifestyle to lead. Worship God with every breath.

⁶Let everything that has breath praise the LORD. Praise the LORD.

Psalm 150:6

mar 11

When perpetual grace interrupts a life devoted to sin, bold steps must be taken to forge a new path that keeps in step with the Spirit.

¹⁷For if, by the trespass of the one man, death reigned through that one man, how much more will those who receive God's abundant provision of grace and of the gift of righteousness reign in life through the one man, Jesus Christ.

Romans 5:17

mar 12

The image of the Church as the Body of Christ is not merely symbolic. Think of the grand implications of being Christ's presence on earth.

²⁷Now you are the body of Christ, and each one of you is a part of it.

1 Corinthians 12:27

mar 13

Sin is obvious. It is not difficult to figure out. Don't make it complicated. If it won't please God just don't do it.

[19]The acts of the sinful nature are obvious: sexual immorality, impurity and debauchery; [20]idolatry and witchcraft; hatred, discord, jealousy, fits of rage, selfish ambition, dissensions, factions [21]and envy; drunkenness, orgies, and the like. I warn you, as I did before, that those who live like this will not inherit the kingdom of God.

Galatians 5:19-21

mar 14

You can pretend you are holy & control almost all of your actions, but if your heart isn't pure your mouth will eventually betray you.

[8]but no man can tame the tongue. It is a restless evil, full of deadly poison.

James 3:8

mar 15

When apathy, lethargy, and hatred take love's rightful place in the believer's heart God's mission is lost and life is wasted.

[14]For Christ's love compels us, because we are convinced that one died for all, and therefore all died.

2 Corinthians 5:14

mar 16

It is sad that arenas are packed to hear what our itching ears long to hear while the Kingdom's great message is often lost in the noise.

[3]For the time will come when men will not put up with sound doctrine. Instead, to suit their own desires, they will gather around them a great number of teachers to say what their itching ears want to hear.

2 Timothy 4:3

mar 17

Measuring a person's worth based on "what they can do for me" reveals our utter incomprehension of the universality of the cross.

²⁸There is neither Jew nor Greek, slave nor free, male nor female, for you are all one in Christ Jesus.

Galatians 3:28

mar 18

Heaven is not the illusionary promise of a distant reward in a faraway place. Eternity is now. We get to establish God's Kingdom on earth.

¹⁰your kingdom come, your will be done on earth as it is in heaven.

Matthew 6:10

53

mar 19

The world is far more interested in your love than your theology (stance on the virgin birth, eternal security, & end-times prophecy).

³⁵By this all men will know that you are my disciples, if you love one another."

John 13:35

mar 20

One of the enemy's greatest strategies is to get Christians to fight on false fronts. Be careful what you fight for and against.

¹²For our struggle is not against flesh and blood, but against the rulers, against the authorities, against the powers of this dark world and against the spiritual forces of evil in the heavenly realms.

Ephesians 6:12

mar 21

Following Jesus can take you places you never wanted to go. But then again, it is more about the company than the destination.

13Greater love has no one than this, that he lay down his life for his friends. 14You are my friends if you do what I command.

John 15:13-14

mar 22

Be careful little mouth what you say. Make certain that the words you speak build up those who listen. Avoid godless chatter.

29Do not let any unwholesome talk come out of your mouths, but only what is helpful for building others up according to their needs, that it may benefit those who listen.

Ephesians 4:29

mar 23

God never promised to keep us from facing trials, but He has promised to go through all of them with us.

⁹if this is so, then the Lord knows how to rescue godly men from trials and to hold the unrighteous for the day of judgment, while continuing their punishment.

2 Peter 2:9

mar 24

Survival mode is where we end up when we refuse to surrender control. God created us to live, not just merely survive.

¹⁰The thief comes only to steal and kill and destroy; I have come that they may have life, and have it to the full.

John 10:10

56

mar 25

We are designed, called, and equipped to reproduce spiritually. Reproduction is what disciples do best.

¹⁴Nevertheless, more and more men and women believed in the Lord and were added to their number.

Acts 5:14

mar 26

What you ask for the most probably reveals what you desire the most. Are you praying for God's will or your own agenda?

⁴²He went away a second time and prayed, "My Father, if it is not possible for this cup to be taken away unless I drink it, may your will be done."

Matthew 26:42

These people we pass by in our cars, wave at in our neighborhoods, & politely chatter with are the very ones we are to share Christ with.

[10]So the servants went out into the streets and gathered all the people they could find, both good and bad, and the wedding hall was filled with guests.

Matthew 22:10

mar 28

All of us are in one of three conditions. We are either dead, dying, or multiplying. Which one best describes you?

[24]I tell you the truth, unless a kernel of wheat falls to the ground and dies, it remains only a single seed. But if it dies, it produces many seeds.

John 12:24

mar 29

God's wisdom provides the perspective, power, and courage to face trails, withstand temptation, & take action. His wisdom is essential.

⁶The mocker seeks wisdom and finds none, but knowledge comes easily to the discerning.

Proverbs 14:6

mar 30

Remove all prejudice from your life. It is not enough to say that we love EVERYONE; we must actively demonstrate our love for EVERYONE.

¹¹Here there is no Greek or Jew, circumcised or uncircumcised, barbarian, Scythian, slave or free, but Christ is all, and is in all.

Colossians 3:11

mar 31

The church is powerful. We do not need to be intimidated nor do we need to bully. Bullying is a weak person's attempt to appear strong.

27Whatever happens, conduct yourselves in a manner worthy of the gospel of Christ. Then, whether I come and see you or only hear about you in my absence, I will know that you stand firm in one spirit, contending as one man for the faith of the gospel 28without being frightened in any way by those who oppose you. This is a sign to them that they will be destroyed, but that you will be saved—and that by God.

Philippians 10:27-28

60

april

61

apr 1

Failing to control your speech will destroy your reputation, reveal hidden indiscretions, and make an utter fool out of you.

⁶The tongue also is a fire, a world of evil among the parts of the body. It corrupts the whole person, sets the whole course of his life on fire, and is itself set on fire by hell.

James 3:6

apr 2

Submission is the key to experiencing true spiritual oneness with God. When we submit to God, the great distractions lose their appeal.

²¹"Submit to God and be at peace with him; in this way prosperity will come to you.

Job 22:21

apr 3

Surrender is counter-intuitive. We are taught to hold on at all costs and never surrender, but letting go is essential to please God.

¹Finally, brothers, we instructed you how to live in order to please God, as in fact you are living. Now we ask you and urge you in the Lord Jesus to do this more and more.

1 Thessalonians 4:1

apr 4

We were created by God with deep relational needs. When those needs are unmet, people experience untold pain and suffering.

¹⁶Turn to me and be gracious to me, for I am lonely and afflicted. ¹⁷The troubles of my heart have multiplied; free me from my anguish.

Psalm 25:16-17

apr 5

One of the great functions of the Church is to eradicate loneliness from the world. Christians must bind themselves relationally to others.

44All the believers were together and had everything in common.

Acts 2:44

apr 6

It is easy to tear others down when you feel bad about yourself. Work hard to be an encourager even in the midst of discouragement.

29Do not let any unwholesome talk come out of your mouths, but only what is helpful for building others up according to their needs, that it may benefit those who listen.

Ephesians 4:29

65

apr 7

People stagnate in their relationship with Christ when they have no one to help them deepen their faith. Find someone to help you grow.

[17]As iron sharpens iron, so one man sharpens another.

Proverbs 27:17

apr 8

Don't worry about all the stuff you don't know, just share the truth you cling to. Jesus is the truth.

[6]Jesus answered, "I am the way and the truth and the life. No one comes to the Father except through me."

John 14:6

An unshared truth can be just as deadly as a spoken lie. People need to hear the truth. Tell them the story of Jesus.

14How, then, can they call on the one they have not believed in? And how can they believe in the one of whom they have not heard? And how can they hear without someone preaching to them?

Romans 10:14

We must recognize that when we reject our calling to serve that our families, our communities, and our churches suffer.

45For even the Son of Man did not come to be served, but to serve, and to give his life as a ransom for many.

Mark 10:45

We are Jesus to the world that we live in. Our communities will see no other Jesus than the one that we present to them.

[16]Let the word of Christ dwell in you richly as you teach and admonish one another with all wisdom, and as you sing psalms, hymns and spiritual songs with gratitude in your hearts to God.

Colossians 3:16

apr 12

There is nothing sicker than the clamoring for power & position that happens among Christians. Humble yourself & serve another.

[14]Now that I, your Lord and Teacher, have washed your feet, you also should wash one another's feet.

John 13:14

apr 13

Worship is the appropriate response to the recognition of God's presence. A heart that has been forgiven by Jesus beats for worship.

²Worship the LORD with gladness; come before him with joyful songs.

Psalm 100:2

apr 14

When worship becomes about your preferences, timetables, agendas, & expectations it is no longer about God & it is no longer worship.

²³Yet a time is coming and has now come when the true worshipers will worship the Father in spirit and truth, for they are the kind of worshipers the Father seeks.

John 4:23

> Worship is not a once a week affair. The transforming power of worship is meant to be experienced daily.

[42]Day after day, in the temple courts and from house to house, they never stopped teaching and proclaiming the good news that Jesus is the Christ.

Acts 5:42

> God is not interested in partial love. He doesn't want your Sundays, occasional quiet times, & sporadic generosity. He wants all of you.

[58]Therefore, my dear brothers, stand firm. Let nothing move you. Always give yourselves fully to the work of the Lord, because you know that your labor in the Lord is not in vain.

1 Corinthians 15:58

apr 17

Followers of Jesus are called to be agents of grace. Christians are to intentionally love people who wrong them.

¹⁴Bless those who persecute you; bless and do not curse.

Romans 12:14

apr 18

God's words are alive and active clamoring to penetrate the heart of every person springing them to new life.

¹²For the word of God is living and active. Sharper than any double-edged sword, it penetrates even to dividing soul and spirit, joints and marrow; it judges the thoughts and attitudes of the heart.

Hebrews 4:12

apr 19

God delivered you, called you, and empowered you to do great and courageous things for the Kingdom. Be strong and very courageous.

[7]Be strong and very courageous. Be careful to obey all the law my servant Moses gave you; do not turn from it to the right or to the left, that you may be successful wherever you go.

Joshua 1:7

---

apr 20

God has a tremendous plan for all of us, but we often lose faith in the face of obstacles and find ourselves adrift in a life void of purpose.

[8]For if you possess these qualities in increasing measure, they will keep you from being ineffective and unproductive in your knowledge of our Lord Jesus Christ.

2 Peter 1:8

apr 21

When we see someone sinning we should not ignore them, nor should we seek to punish them. We should take them by the hand & lift them up.

²²Be merciful to those who doubt; ²³snatch others from the fire and save them; to others show mercy, mixed with fear—hating even the clothing stained by corrupted flesh.

Jude 1:22-23

apr 22

Judging others typically creates an atmosphere of fear & bondage as those who judge go to greater and greater lengths to hide their own sin.

¹Do not judge, or you too will be judged. ²For in the same way you judge others, you will be judged, and with the measure you use, it will be measured to you.

Matthew 7:1-2

73

apr 23

Do the good in every situation. Do what is right even when it costs you. Others may get ahead today, but you will thrive for eternity.

⁹Let us not become weary in doing good, for at the proper time we will reap a harvest if we do not give up.

Galatians 6:9

---

apr 24

God calls us to be love initiators. He says us to love unreasonably by not resisting those who try take advantage of us & to bless them as well.

⁴⁰And if someone wants to sue you and take your tunic, let him have your cloak as well. ⁴¹If someone forces you to go one mile, go with him two miles. ⁴²Give to the one who asks you, and do not turn away from the one who wants to borrow from you.

Matthew 5:40-42

apr 25

Worry is driven by misplaced priorities. Jesus says that if we seek Him first, that there is nothing left to worry about.

³³But seek first his kingdom and his righteousness, and all these things will be given to you as well. ³⁴Therefore do not worry about tomorrow, for tomorrow will worry about itself. Each day has enough trouble of its own.

Matthew 6:33-34

apr 26

It is crazy to claim that you trust God with your eternal well-being while refusing to trust Him with the issues you face each day.

⁷The LORD is my strength and my shield; my heart trusts in him, and I am helped. My heart leaps for joy and I will give thanks to him in song.

Psalm 28:7

apr 27

When you leave God behind and try to take matters into your own hands you end up stressed, panicked, & exhausted.

³In the morning, O LORD, you hear my voice; in the morning I lay my requests before you and wait in expectation.

Psalm 5:3

apr 28

Dependency upon God is the only path to true abundance. Seeking Him first places us in the direct stream of His provision.

³³But seek first his kingdom and his righteousness, and all these things will be given to you as well.

Matthew 6:33

apr 29

Not only are we to be recipients of the Kingdom of Heaven, we are also to become participants in building the Kingdom. What a privilege!

¹⁷Therefore, if anyone is in Christ, he is a new creation; the old has gone, the new has come! ¹⁸All this is from God, who reconciled us to himself through Christ and gave us the ministry of reconciliation: ¹⁹that God was reconciling the world to himself in Christ, not counting men's sins against them. And he has committed to us the message of reconciliation.

2 Corinthians 5:17-19

apr 30

The world is in a constant state of decay. It desperately needs preserving & Jesus declared that we are the salt of the world.

¹³You are the salt of the earth. But if the salt loses its saltiness, how can it be made salty again? It is no longer good for anything, except to be thrown out and trampled by men.

Matthew 5:13

may

may 1

Jesus does the hard stuff. He fulfills the Law & removes sin. All we need to do is accept our new identity & lead lives of love.

⁸For it is by grace you have been saved, through faith—and this not from yourselves, it is the gift of God— ⁹not by works, so that no one can boast.

Ephesians 2:8-9

may 2

We think that we can direct hatred, but hatred is so powerful that it always has a residual impact. Unchecked hatred eventually consumes us.

¹²Hatred stirs up dissension, but love covers over all wrongs.

Proverbs 10:12

81

may 3

The mere appearance of piety holds little hope for authentic satisfaction, but discrete action to please God leads to lasting soul satisfaction.

[1]Be careful not to do your 'acts of righteousness' before men, to be seen by them. If you do, you will have no reward from your Father in heaven.

Matthew 6:1

may 4

Put your money where your heart is, because if you don't your heart will stray. A misplaced treasure leads to an empty heart.

[21]For where your treasure is, there your heart will be also.

Matthew 6:21

may 5

When we treasure the eternal we store up eternal reward. The things of God will never lose their appeal, depreciate, break, or decay.

¹⁹Do not store up for yourselves treasures on earth, where moth and rust destroy, and where thieves break in and steal. ²⁰But store up for yourselves treasures in heaven, where moth and rust do not destroy, and where thieves do not break in and steal.

Matthew 6:19-20

may 6

The best expression of freedom is love. The worst is sin. Love sets others free while sin enslaves. Use your freedom as God intends.

¹³You, my brothers, were called to be free. But do not use your freedom to indulge the sinful nature; rather, serve one another in love.

Galatians 5:13

may 7

Materialism is slavery. We become shackled by the material things of this world when God clearly wants us to be liberated by His Spirit.

[24]No one can serve two masters. Either he will hate the one and love the other, or he will be devoted to the one and despise the other. You cannot serve both God and Money.

Matthew 6:24

may 8

This is the one and only life any of us will ever live. We must take extreme measures to ensure what we are building will last.

[24]"Therefore everyone who hears these words of mine and puts them into practice is like a wise man who built his house on the rock. [25]The rain came down, the streams rose, and the winds blew and beat against that house; yet it did not fall, because it had its foundation on the rock. [26]But everyone who hears these words of mine and does not put them into practice is like a foolish man who built his house on sand. [27]The rain came down, the streams rose, and the winds blew and beat against that house, and it fell with a great crash."

Matthew 7:24-27

may 9

Salvation is a daily process of death & rebirth. It is crucial that we die to self everyday & surrender to God's will.

²⁵The man who loves his life will lose it, while the man who hates his life in this world will keep it for eternal life. ²⁶Whoever serves me must follow me; and where I am, my servant also will be. My Father will honor the one who serves me.

John 12:25-26

may 10

God's eternal perspective shows that everything is radically different from how we view it from within the confines of this world.

⁹As the heavens are higher than the earth, so are my ways higher than your ways and my thoughts than your thoughts.

Isaiah 55:9

may 11

Striving to be first leads to frustration, exhaustion, & destruction because the only path to true eternal success is found in being last.

³¹"But many who are first will be last, and the last first."

Mark 10:31

may 12

When we drop our agendas & put God's will first, we leave numerous things behind as we live to build God's Kingdom instead of our own.

²⁹"I tell you the truth," Jesus replied, "no one who has left home or brothers or sisters or mother or father or children or fields for me and the gospel ³⁰will fail to receive a hundred times as much in this present age (homes, brothers, sisters, mothers, children and fields—and with them, persecutions) and in the age to come, eternal life.

Mark 10:29-30

may 13

We find prestige and honor in being served, but God says that prestige and honor can only be found through being a servant.

⁴³Not so with you. Instead, whoever wants to become great among you must be your servant.

Mark 10:43

may 14

If you are looking to store up eternal riches, then giving is the strategy for you. Giving wealth now leads to great treasures forever.

¹⁸Command them to do good, to be rich in good deeds, and to be generous and willing to share. ¹⁹In this way they will lay up treasure for themselves as a firm foundation for the coming age, so that they may take hold of the life that is truly life.

1 Timothy 6:18-19

We must never forget that we GET to give. God doesn't need our money, time, or efforts. Giving is a privilege.

[35]In everything I did, I showed you that by this kind of hard work we must help the weak, remembering the words the Lord Jesus himself said: 'It is more blessed to give than to receive.'

Acts 20:35

If giving brings God pleasure then those who are united with Him will find great blessing in it as well. The godly will give generously.

[7]Each man should give what he has decided in his heart to give, not reluctantly or under compulsion, for God loves a cheerful giver.

2 Corinthians 9:7

may 17

Giving unites us with the heart & purpose of Christ & allows us to transcend the trappings of this world. Don't be afraid to give.

⁹A generous man will himself be blessed, for he shares his food with the poor.

Proverbs 22:9

may 18

All of us are slaves to something. We are either slaves to sin or slaves to righteousness. One master leads to death the other to life.

¹⁷But thanks be to God that, though you used to be slaves to sin, you wholeheartedly obeyed the form of teaching to which you were entrusted. ¹⁸You have been set free from sin and have become slaves to righteousness.

Romans 6:17-18

may 19

Christ purchased us on the cross so that we could be truly free. The burden of sin is lifted & we are free to live as God intended.

¹It is for freedom that Christ has set us free. Stand firm, then, and do not let yourselves be burdened again by a yoke of slavery.

Galatians 5:1

may 20

Many people love the idea of Jesus as Savior, yet despise the thought of Jesus as Lord. You cannot have one without the other.

²²But now that you have been set free from sin and have become slaves to God, the benefit you reap leads to holiness, and the result is eternal life.

Romans 6:22

may 21

This world tells us that strength is found in power and control, but in God's economy strength is best found in weakness.

⁹But he said to me, "My grace is sufficient for you, for my power is made perfect in weakness." Therefore I will boast all the more gladly about my weaknesses, so that Christ's power may rest on me.

2 Corinthians 12:9

may 22

Those who are strong in this world often have the greatest difficulty allowing God to use them, because they rely on their own strength.

⁹Indeed, in our hearts we felt the sentence of death. But this happened that we might not rely on ourselves but on God, who raises the dead.

2 Corinthians 1:9

may 23

God uses us not only in spite of our weaknesses, but also in the midst of them. His power is best displayed against a backdrop of weakness.

[27]But God chose the foolish things of the world to shame the wise; God chose the weak things of the world to shame the strong.

1 Corinthians 1:27

may 24

God is love; therefore all true love must originate with Him. We are only capable of love when we are connected to the source of love.

[7]Dear friends, let us love one another, for love comes from God. Everyone who loves has been born of God and knows God. [8]Whoever does not love does not know God, because God is love.

1 John 4:7-8

There are fans of Jesus & there are disciples of Jesus. Fans sit on the sideline & cheer Him on. Disciples get in the game & do His work.

[34]"A new command I give you: Love one another. As I have loved you, so you must love one another. [35]By this all men will know that you are my disciples, if you love one another."

John 13:34-35

may 26

We love because we have received love & love demands to be shared. When you know God, you can't help but to love others.

[16]And so we know and rely on the love God has for us. God is love. Whoever lives in love lives in God, and God in him.

1 John 4:16

93

may 27

Understanding salvation begins with accepting that it is initiated, provided, and maintained by God. It is His to give not ours to earn.

⁶You see, at just the right time, when we were still powerless, Christ died for the ungodly.

Romans 5:6

may 28

Circumstantial joy is blown away with every bitter wind, but steady are the emotions of the one anchored by faith in Him.

⁴Rejoice in the Lord always. I will say it again: Rejoice!

Philippians 4:4

may 29

Don't let your life be a waste. Your life matters so get off of the couch & do something with it. God created you for a grand purpose.

⁶I pray that you may be active in sharing your faith, so that you will have a full understanding of every good thing we have in Christ.

Philemon 1:6

may 30

The end is near, but it is not too late. Do something great with your one and only life.

⁷The end of all things is near. Therefore be clear minded and self-controlled so that you can pray.

1 Peter 4:7

Prayer is not about convincing God to do your will, but aligning yourself to His will.

⁴Show me your ways, O LORD, teach me your paths;

Psalm 25:4

june

jun 1

Less is more. When less of you is in the way, more of God is revealed through you. Become less so He is seen more.

³⁰He must become greater; I must become less.

John 3:30

jun 2

From the beginning God's desire was for your identity to be totally wrapped up in who He is. You were created in His image to know Him.

²⁶Then God said, "Let us make man in our image, in our likeness, and let them rule over the fish of the sea and the birds of the air, over the livestock, over all the earth, and over all the creatures that move along the ground."

Genesis 1:26

jun 3

In Christ you find an identity that cannot be stolen, lost, broken or destroyed because it is based on one eternal truth: You are His.

²¹Now it is God who makes both us and you stand firm in Christ. He anointed us, ²²set his seal of ownership on us, and put his Spirit in our hearts as a deposit, guaranteeing what is to come.

2 Corinthians 1:21-22

jun 4

You are a loved, chosen and set-apart child of the almighty God. You were created on purpose for a purpose.

⁸The LORD will fulfill his purpose for me; your love, O LORD, endures forever— do not abandon the works of your hands.

Psalm 138:8

jun 5

We have this perception that love will just kind of take care of itself, but it doesn't. Love requires work and dedication.

[12]Because of the increase of wickedness, the love of most will grow cold, [13]but he who stands firm to the end will be saved.

Matthew 24:12-13

jun 6

In letting go of the only life we know, we are caught and held by the only Life there is. We must lose our lives to find life.

[35]For whoever wants to save his life will lose it, but whoever loses his life for me and for the gospel will save it.

Mark 8:35

101

jun 7

> We are saved by God from God for God. Salvation is not to be wasted. Live as though you are saved.

³⁶Whoever believes in the Son has eternal life, but whoever rejects the Son will not see life, for God's wrath remains on him."

John 3:36

---

jun 8

> Salvation is not about living to die, it is about dying to live. Die to self so that you are free to live abundantly.

¹³For if you live according to the sinful nature, you will die; but if by the Spirit you put to death the misdeeds of the body, you will live, ¹⁴because those who are led by the Spirit of God are sons of God.

Romans 8:13-14

jun 9

> Avoid the sin of comparison. Relative holiness has no value. Being better than the average Christian is not our goal. Being like Christ is.

³If anyone thinks he is something when he is nothing, he deceives himself. ⁴Each one should test his own actions. Then he can take pride in himself, without comparing himself to somebody else.

Galatians 6:3-4

jun 10

> Following Jesus is not a cake walk proposition. It is more like a treacherous hike up a mountain pass with no guarantee of personal safety.

¹³But rejoice that you participate in the sufferings of Christ, so that you may be overjoyed when his glory is revealed.

1 Peter 4:13

jun 11

Entitlement is the great deception of our time. If God loves me I will be healthy, wealthy, & better than everybody else. It's a brutal lie.

⁶Their visions are false and their divinations a lie. They say, "The LORD declares," when the LORD has not sent them; yet they expect their words to be fulfilled.

Ezekiel 13:6

jun 12

Don't strive for 1st or 2nd. Those come far too easy. 3rd place is our goal, but we often get ahead of ourselves. Love God. Love others.

³Do nothing out of selfish ambition or vain conceit, but in humility consider others better than yourselves.

Philippians 2:3

jun 13

Human conflict is merely the outward manifestation of the absence of inner peace. Make peace with God & you can have peace with man.

⁷When a man's ways are pleasing to the LORD, he makes even his enemies live at peace with him.

Proverbs 16:7

jun 14

Security can never be obtained through the shaky circumstantial world we live in. Clinging to the eternal is our only hope.

¹⁹We have this hope as an anchor for the soul, firm and secure.

Hebrews 6:19a

105

jun 15

In the midst of chaos God is in control. Breathe deep and fix your mind on Him. He can calm the waters of your soul.

¹Therefore, holy brothers, who share in the heavenly calling, fix your thoughts on Jesus, the apostle and high priest whom we confess.

Hebrews 3:1

jun 16

Our refusal to lay our burdens down slows us so much that eventually Jesus is nothing more than a tiny dot on the distant horizon.

²⁸"Come to me, all you who are weary and burdened, and I will give you rest. ²⁹Take my yoke upon you and learn from me, for I am gentle and humble in heart, and you will find rest for your souls. ³⁰For my yoke is easy and my burden is light."

Matthew 11:28-30

Many hope to make a treaty with the Truth. You know, divide their life in half. But the Truth is greedy. Not stopping until He conquers all.

⁵Or do you think Scripture says without reason that the spirit he caused to live in us envies intensely?

James 4:5

Salvation moves you from death to life, turns you from a sinner into a saint, and takes you from depravity into holiness.

¹²But when this priest had offered for all time one sacrifice for sins, he sat down at the right hand of God. ¹³Since that time he waits for his enemies to be made his footstool, ¹⁴because by one sacrifice he has made perfect forever those who are being made holy.

Hebrews 10:12-14

jun 19

Meeting with God is often less about what we receive from Him and more about what he removes from us.

²But who can endure the day of his coming? Who can stand when he appears? For he will be like a refiner's fire or a launderer's soap.

Malachi 3:2

jun 20

"Acting" like a Christian can be done on your own strength and ability but to actually follow Jesus requires a drastic desperation for Him.

²⁷"Woe to you, teachers of the law and Pharisees, you hypocrites! You are like whitewashed tombs, which look beautiful on the outside but on the inside are full of dead men's bones and everything unclean.

Matthew 23:27

jun 21

In the name of reverence and propriety, the transforming power of Jesus is often replaced with a manual for conformity.

²Do not conform any longer to the pattern of this world, but be transformed by the renewing of your mind. Then you will be able to test and approve what God's will is—his good, pleasing and perfect will.

Romans 12:2

jun 22

There are only two kinds of people in this world: Those who are in recovery and those who need to be in recovery.

¹¹Again I ask: Did they stumble so as to fall beyond recovery? Not at all! Rather, because of their transgression, salvation has come to the Gentiles to make Israel envious.

Romans 11:11

jun 23

> If your faith is easy, safe and trouble-free then it probably isn't faith in Jesus. Faith in Jesus is usually wildly unsettling.

²⁶I have been constantly on the move. I have been in danger from rivers, in danger from bandits, in danger from my own countrymen, in danger from Gentiles; in danger in the city, in danger in the country, in danger at sea; and in danger from false brothers.

2 Corinthians 11:26

jun 24

> Obedience to God changes the world. Disobedience perpetuates the ho-hum. Are you a world changer or a ho-hummer?

¹³Because of the service by which you have proved yourselves, men will praise God for the obedience that accompanies your confession of the gospel of Christ, and for your generosity in sharing with them and with everyone else.

2 Corinthians 9:13

> God's desire is to lead a wildly diverse body of misfits on a rambunctious relational journey of epic proportions. Now that's Church!

26Brothers, think of what you were when you were called. Not many of you were wise by human standards; not many were influential; not many were of noble birth. 27But God chose the foolish things of the world to shame the wise; God chose the weak things of the world to shame the strong.

1 Corinthians 1:26-27

> Normalcy is a man-made illusion that prevents the majority of us from reaching our God-given potential. God did not create normal people.

4There are different kinds of gifts, but the same Spirit. 5There are different kinds of service, but the same Lord. 6There are different kinds of working, but the same God works all of them in all men.

1 Corinthians 12:4-6

The road to mediocrity is paved with normalcy. Our attempts to be normal rob the world of experiencing the greatness of God's creation.

¹⁸But in fact God has arranged the parts in the body, every one of them, just as he wanted them to be. ¹⁹If they were all one part, where would the body be? ²⁰As it is, there are many parts, but one body.

1 Corinthians 12:18-20

Sacrifice is giving until it hurts. If you cannot feel your giving it isn't sacrificial. What are you sacrificing to build God's Kingdom?

⁵you also, like living stones, are being built into a spiritual house to be a holy priesthood, offering spiritual sacrifices acceptable to God through Jesus Christ.

1 Peter 2:5

jun 29

The tyranny of the urgent can be overthrown. Time holds no power for the eternally aware. We CAN do the things that really matter.

²because through Christ Jesus the law of the Spirit of life set me free from the law of sin and death.

Romans 8:2

jun 30

Danglers never change the world. You must let go to be a world-changer. Surrender is crucial to keep in step with the Holy Spirit.

²⁵Since we live by the Spirit, let us keep in step with the Spirit.

Galatians 5:25

july

jul 1

Delayed obedience is disobedience. You are in conflict with the will of God until you submit. Why fight a battle you can't win?

17For the sinful nature desires what is contrary to the Spirit, and the Spirit what is contrary to the sinful nature. They are in conflict with each other, so that you do not do what you want.

Galatians 5:17

jul 2

It is impossible to return to a former state of spirituality. Don't go back. Just move forward & pursue consistent steady growth.

12Not that I have already obtained all this, or have already been made perfect, but I press on to take hold of that for which Christ Jesus took hold of me.

Philippians 3:12

> God gives us the mountain to prepare us for life in the valley. Remember the mountain, but don't miss the experience of the valley.

⁴Even though I walk through the valley of the shadow of death, I will fear no evil, for you are with me; your rod and your staff, they comfort me.

Psalm 23:4

> When churches compete with each other nobody wins. There are plenty of lost people to go around. Christians are the rare commodity.

⁸For God, who was at work in the ministry of Peter as an apostle to the Jews, was also at work in my ministry as an apostle to the Gentiles. ⁹James, Peter and John, those reputed to be pillars, gave me and Barnabas the right hand of fellowship when they recognized the grace given to me. They agreed that we should go to the Gentiles, and they to the Jews.

Galatians 2:8-9

jul 5

It is better by far to offend the "godly" to reach the lost, than appease the "godly" and lose the lost.

¹¹When Peter came to Antioch, I opposed him to his face, because he was clearly in the wrong. ¹²Before certain men came from James, he used to eat with the Gentiles. But when they arrived, he began to draw back and separate himself from the Gentiles because he was afraid of those who belonged to the circumcision group. ¹³The other Jews joined him in his hypocrisy, so that by their hypocrisy even Barnabas was led astray.

Galatians 2:11-13

jul 6

Churches will make mistakes, but when we err it better be on the side of reaching out too aggressively (if that is even possible).

²⁸We proclaim him, admonishing and teaching everyone with all wisdom, so that we may present everyone perfect in Christ. ²⁹To this end I labor, struggling with all his energy, which so powerfully works in me.

Colossians 1:28-29

jul 7

Everything is better than it seems. No matter how difficult the present is, the future holds the promise of the restoration of all things.

¹³But in keeping with his promise we are looking forward to a new heaven and a new earth, the home of righteousness.

2 Peter 3:13

jul 8

We do not dictate where God will lead us. We simply follow the path that He cuts even when it is the last place we want to go.

⁹In his heart a man plans his course, but the LORD determines his steps.

Proverbs 16:9

jul 9

Leadership is not breaking the spirit but is setting it free to run.

³²I run in the path of your commands, for you have set my heart free.

Psalm 119:32

jul 10

The glory of God is reflected & magnified in us. We are walking neon signs proclaiming the goodness, grace, & love of the almighty Creator.

⁶For God, who said, "Let light shine out of darkness," made his light shine in our hearts to give us the light of the knowledge of the glory of God in the face of Christ.

2 Corinthians 4:6

Satan lures many into subtle submission by keeping them fixated on the physical realm. They are unaware of the spiritual battle that rages.

8Be self-controlled and alert. Your enemy the devil prowls around like a roaring lion looking for someone to devour.

1 Peter 5:8

Satan's agenda is simple…to keep you unproductive. If you aren't in the fight, you are already defeated.

8Produce fruit in keeping with repentance.

Matthew 3:8

jul 13

Ultimately Jesus wins, so no matter what, we are strong beyond measure. Weakness is a choice that no Christian should ever accept.

⁴You, dear children, are from God and have overcome them, because the one who is in you is greater than the one who is in the world.

1 John 4:4

jul 14

An emotionless Christian is a dead Christian. When we stop hurting with those who hurt, we no longer have the heart beat of Jesus.

¹⁵Rejoice with those who rejoice; mourn with those who mourn.

Romans 12:15

123

When we no longer grieve over the story of the cross or get goose bumps at the thought of the resurrection, we have grown cold and lifeless.

[20]After he said this, he showed them his hands and side. The disciples were overjoyed when they saw the Lord.

John 20:20

We often get consumed with the temporal as the eternal things of God go undone. We think that eternity can wait, but it can't & it doesn't.

[13]his work will be shown for what it is, because the Day will bring it to light. It will be revealed with fire, and the fire will test the quality of each man's work.

1 Corinthians 3:13

jul 17

You are responsible for what you know. Whatever you have learned about Jesus, you need to pass onto others.

³We proclaim to you what we have seen and heard, so that you also may have fellowship with us. And our fellowship is with the Father and with his Son, Jesus Christ.

1 John 1:3

jul 18

It is unacceptable to sit in church your whole life being fed & never teach anyone else. Find someone who knows less then you & teach them.

²Preach the Word; be prepared in season and out of season; correct, rebuke and encourage—with great patience and careful instruction.

2 Timothy 4:2

jul 19

It is tempting to hold onto past hurts as a form of present protection, but maintaining festering wounds prevents us from following Jesus.

¹³Brothers, I do not consider myself yet to have taken hold of it. But one thing I do: Forgetting what is behind and straining toward what is ahead, ¹⁴I press on toward the goal to win the prize for which God has called me heavenward in Christ Jesus.

Philippians 3:13-14

jul 20

As long as we hold firmly to the sinner's mentality we are never truly free to live as saints. Let go of sin for we have been transformed.

¹⁷Therefore, if anyone is in Christ, he is a new creation; the old has gone, the new has come!

2 Corinthians 5:17

jul 21

> When we hold onto grudges and refuse to offer forgiveness to those who have hurt us, we purposefully do not act like Jesus.

¹⁸Do not seek revenge or bear a grudge against one of your people, but love your neighbor as yourself. I am the LORD.

Leviticus 19:18

jul 22

> The problem with punishing ourselves is that we don't know when to stop. If Jesus can forgive us, shouldn't we forgive ourselves?

²²let us draw near to God with a sincere heart in full assurance of faith, having our hearts sprinkled to cleanse us from a guilty conscience and having our bodies washed with pure water.

Hebrews 10:22

jul 23

God is doing a new thing with you. The old has gone. The new has come. God has done away with the past & He is ushering in a new reality.

¹⁹See, I am doing a new thing! Now it springs up; do you not perceive it? I am making a way in the desert and streams in the wasteland.

Isaiah 43:19

jul 24

Stop dwelling on the turmoil of the past. Let it go so that you can hold onto and dwell in God's perfect peace.

¹²Fight the good fight of the faith. Take hold of the eternal life to which you were called when you made your good confession in the presence of many witnesses.

1 Timothy 6:12

The human soul does not have the capacity to hold a warring past & a peaceful present at the same time. You must choose one or the other.

27Peace I leave with you; my peace I give you. I do not give to you as the world gives. Do not let your hearts be troubled and do not be afraid.

John 14:27

Behavioral change flows out of identity acceptance. We accept what God has done at the core of our being & a new reality takes hold.

3But among you there must not be even a hint of sexual immorality, or of any kind of impurity, or of greed, because these are improper for God's holy people.

Ephesians 5:3

Authentic transformation is birthed in pain. We outgrow the cocoon of self as we blossom into magnificent new creations.

³Not only so, but we also rejoice in our sufferings, because we know that suffering produces perseverance; ⁴perseverance, character; and character, hope. ⁵And hope does not disappoint us, because God has poured out his love into our hearts by the Holy Spirit, whom he has given us.

Romans 5:3-5

jul 28

When we place our faith in material wealth instead of God, we are robbed of the abundant life God so generously provides.

¹⁰I denied myself nothing my eyes desired; I refused my heart no pleasure. My heart took delight in all my work, and this was the reward for all my labor. ¹¹Yet when I surveyed all that my hands had done and what I had toiled to achieve, everything was meaningless, a chasing after the wind; nothing was gained under the sun.

Ecclesiastes 2:10-11

jul 29

Recognizing that God is the provider of all things is a crucial perspective to posses. It is also one of the easiest perspectives to lose.

[17]Command those who are rich in this present world not to be arrogant nor to put their hope in wealth, which is so uncertain, but to put their hope in God, who richly provides us with everything for our enjoyment.

1 Timothy 6:17

jul 30

Sacrifice is giving until it hurts. God's desire is that we would be generous and generosity only occurs when we sacrifice.

[14]"Cursed is the cheat who has an acceptable male in his flock and vows to give it, but then sacrifices a blemished animal to the Lord. For I am a great king," says the LORD Almighty, "and my name is to be feared among the nations.

Malachi 1:14

Whatever you put your trust in will become your god. It will be your master and will determine your actions.

[24]No one can serve two masters. Either he will hate the one and love the other, or he will be devoted to the one and despise the other. You cannot serve both God and Money.

Matthew 6:24

august

aug 1

Jesus made right, through his death, what we are powerless to do. Jesus atoned for our sin by putting our sin to death in His body.

¹⁸For Christ died for sins once for all, the righteous for the unrighteous, to bring you to God. He was put to death in the body but made alive by the Spirit.

1 Peter 3:18

aug 2

Sin is anything done that God has forbidden or anything undone that God has commanded. Sin isn't difficult to figure out. Sin is no mystery.

¹⁹The acts of the sinful nature are obvious: sexual immorality, impurity and debauchery;

Galatians 5:19

135

Sin is a universal problem. It impacts everyone and everything. Sin ushered DEATH into this world and death touches us all.

[12]Therefore, just as sin entered the world through one man, and death through sin, and in this way death came to all men, because all sinned.

Romans 5:12

No doubt about it, you will experience one two realities in your lifetime...You will die or Jesus will come back. Either way, the end is near.

[20]He who testifies to these things says, "Yes, I am coming soon." Amen. Come, Lord Jesus.

Revelation 22:20

aug 5

We always think that tomorrow will come, but one day tomorrow won't come. Are you ready for that day?

²for you know very well that the day of the Lord will come like a thief in the night.

1 Thessalonians 5:2

aug 6

The great question about the return of Jesus is not "if Jesus is coming back" or even "when Jesus is coming back", but "are you ready".

⁴But you, brothers, are not in darkness so that this day should surprise you like a thief. ⁵You are all sons of the light and sons of the day. We do not belong to the night or to the darkness. ⁶So then, let us not be like others, who are asleep, but let us be alert and self-controlled.

1 Thessalonians 5:4-6

137

aug 7

Where there's regret, Jesus provides forgiveness. Where there's sorrow, Jesus gives hope. Where there's longing, Jesus provides fulfillment.

³His divine power has given us everything we need for life and godliness through our knowledge of him who called us by his own glory and goodness.

2 Peter 1:3

aug 8

Time is a constraint for the hopelessly mortal. It sets identity & purpose on when & where while the hopeful eternal are free to simply be.

¹¹He has made everything beautiful in its time. He has also set eternity in the hearts of men; yet they cannot fathom what God has done from beginning to end.

Ecclesiastes 3:11

Want to change your city? Love the people. God placed you in your city to be His ambassador & to carry out His ministry of reconciliation.

⁴¹As he approached Jerusalem and saw the city, he wept over it ⁴²and said, "If you, even you, had only known on this day what would bring you peace—but now it is hidden from your eyes.

Luke 19:41-42

aug 10

When you live a holy life within your community, God's blessing extends to those around you. We bring blessing by obeying Christ.

¹¹Through the blessing of the upright a city is exalted, but by the mouth of the wicked it is destroyed.

Proverbs 11:11

aug 11

A cheerful giver is one who experiences transformation at the core of their being. Generosity is the expression of inward transformation.

[7]Each man should give what he has decided in his heart to give, not reluctantly or under compulsion, for God loves a cheerful giver.

2 Corinthians 9:7

aug 12

Sufficiency is not achieved through independence, but through an utter dependency on God. Sufficiency is never found apart from God.

[8]And God is able to make all grace abound to you, so that in all things at all times, having all that you need, you will abound in every good work.

2 Corinthians 9:8

aug 13

Giving sets us free from the lie of self-sufficiency and positions us appropriately in God's economy of generous sowing and reaping.

¹⁰Now he who supplies seed to the sower and bread for food will also supply and increase your store of seed and will enlarge the harvest of your righteousness.

2 Corinthians 9:10

aug 14

Giving causes people to worship. They rejoice in the provision & give glory to God. When we give we become worship initiators.

¹¹You will be made rich in every way so that you can be generous on every occasion, and through us your generosity will result in thanksgiving to God.

2 Corinthians 9:11

aug 15

Many people have an attraction to God. They like the idea of God. They feel a fondness for Him, but that is not enough. Love is required.

[12]No one has ever seen God; but if we love one another, God lives in us and his love is made complete in us.

1 John 4:12

aug 16

Once a person is infected by God's love they become carriers. They pass the love of God onto others, because love is contagious.

[19]We love because he first loved us.

1 John 4:19

aug 17

Anger is not always sinful. It becomes a problem when we allow it to control our actions. Unchecked expressions of anger NEVER honor God.

[19]My dear brothers, take note of this: Everyone should be quick to listen, slow to speak and slow to become angry, [20]for man's anger does not bring about the righteous life that God desires.

James 1:19-20

aug 18

Holding onto anger will impact every relationship you have. Anger is impossible to direct. It will overflow into every avenue of your life.

[26]"In your anger do not sin": Do not let the sun go down while you are still angry, [27]and do not give the devil a foothold.

So true!

Ephesians 4:26-27

143

aug 19

Anger is generally expressed in destructive ways. Whether passive-aggressive or plain old aggressive-aggressive, it's still destructive.

²⁹Do not let any unwholesome talk come out of your mouths, but only what is helpful for building others up according to their needs, that it may benefit those who listen. ³⁰And do not grieve the Holy Spirit of God, with whom you were sealed for the day of redemption. ³¹Get rid of all bitterness, rage and anger, brawling and slander, along with every form of malice.

Ephesians 4:29-31

---

aug 20

Deny forgiveness and you will be a slave to anger. Extend grace to others and anger will not stand a chance.

³²Be kind and compassionate to one another, forgiving each other, just as in Christ God forgave you.

Ephesians 4:32

aug 21

Never forget who you were before coming to know Christ. There is no room for arrogance in the heart of the truly redeemed.

3All of us also lived among them at one time, gratifying the cravings of our sinful nature and following its desires and thoughts. Like the rest, we were by nature objects of wrath.

Ephesians 2:3

aug 22

Whatever our loss, whatever our sorrow, completeness and restoration is a present day reality through the salvation of Jesus Christ.

5But I trust in your unfailing love; my heart rejoices in your salvation.

Psalm 13:5

aug 23

Fixing our minds on salvation provides a constant reminder that Jesus is enough. We do not need Jesus plus anything. He is sufficient.

⁹Then my soul will rejoice in the LORD and delight in his salvation.

Psalm 35:9

aug 24

Salvation brings joy. Joy forces out sorrow as we realize that even our greatest losses can never compare to what we have gained in Christ.

¹²Restore to me the joy of your salvation and grant me a willing spirit, to sustain me.

Psalm 51:12

aug 25

Worship positions us to move beyond on our sorrows. When we sing to Him, we are flooded with poetic remembrances of His mighty works.

⁶I will sing to the LORD, for he has been good to me.

Psalm 13:6

aug 26

God wants us to understand His spiritual gifts. He wants us to utilize our gifts while encouraging others to fully express theirs.

¹Now about spiritual gifts, brothers, I do not want you to be ignorant.

1 Corinthians 12:1

147

aug 27

Trust fund babies have nothing on you. The privileged few who inherit great wealth receive nothing compared to the riches we have in Jesus.

⁷So you are no longer a slave, but a son; and since you are a son, God has made you also an heir.

Galatians 4:7

aug 28

We use "Messiah Complex" to criticize people who act holier than thou. What if we had true messiah complexes & actually lived like Jesus?

²⁴"A student is not above his teacher, nor a servant above his master. ²⁵It is enough for the student to be like his teacher, and the servant like his master.

Matthew 10:24-25a

aug 29

Human vengeance always goes too far. It escalates & sets a pattern wrong-doing in motion bringing untold pain & suffering upon humanity.

¹⁷Do not repay anyone evil for evil. Be careful to do what is right in the eyes of everybody.

Romans 12:17

aug 30

Evil is never defeated with evil. Responding hatefully to someone who wrongs you only escalates the problem & continues the cycle of hatred.

²¹Do not be overcome by evil, but overcome evil with good.

Romans 12:21

The quiet desperation of authentic surrender is best experienced in calloused knees, clean hands, & ready feet.

[1]I urge, then, first of all, that requests, prayers, intercession and thanksgiving be made for everyone— [2]for kings and all those in authority, that we may live peaceful and quiet lives in all godliness and holiness. [3]This is good, and pleases God our Savior, [4]who wants all men to be saved and to come to a knowledge of the truth.

1 Timothy 2:1-4

september

sep 1

Stay away from the pseudo, social, feel good gospels of our day. They are empty & powerless claiming promises Jesus never made.

³⁰since you are going through the same struggle you saw I had, and now hear that I still have.

Philippians 1:30

sep 2

It is impossible to reflect the glory of God when our faces are veiled in selfishness. Remove all that overshadows the light of Jesus.

¹⁸And we, who with unveiled faces all reflect the Lord's glory, are being transformed into his likeness with ever-increasing glory, which comes from the Lord, who is the Spirit.

2 Corinthians 3:18

153

sep 3

The true gift isn't that we are saved, but that we LIVE. If we don't live out our salvation, then we have not received what God intended.

¹²Therefore, my dear friends, as you have always obeyed—not only in my presence, but now much more in my absence— continue to work out your salvation with fear and trembling.

Philippians 2:12

sep 4

God isn't a cosmic deity dispenser passing out little hits of Jesus. When He gives His Holy Spirit we're filled completely. He's sufficient.

¹⁶I pray that out of his glorious riches he may strengthen you with power through his Spirit in your inner being, ¹⁷so that Christ may dwell in your hearts through faith. And I pray that you, being rooted and established in love, ¹⁸may have power, together with all the saints, to grasp how wide and long and high and deep is the love of Christ.

Ephesians 3:16-18

sep 5

When we dwell in righteousness there is no shame. It is an amazing realization of true liberation when we are clean before God.

[15]so that you may become blameless and pure, children of God without fault in a crooked and depraved generation, in which you shine like stars in the universe.

Philippians 2:15

sep 6

Our message is clear. We tell the world that Jesus came, He lived in perfection, He died receiving our sin inside of Him, & He rose again.

[16]as you hold out the word of life—in order that I may boast on the day of Christ that I did not run or labor for nothing.

Philippians 2:16

sep 7

The Creator determines the purpose of His creation and God's purpose for you is to be intimately united to Him.

[10]For if, when we were God's enemies, we were reconciled to him through the death of his Son, how much more, having been reconciled, shall we be saved through his life!

Romans 5:10

---

sep 8

The easily offended struggle mightily to follow Jesus because He tends to lead us in the direct path of those we find most offensive.

[30]But the Pharisees and the teachers of the law who belonged to their sect complained to his disciples, "Why do you eat and drink with tax collectors and 'sinners'?" [31]Jesus answered them, "It is not the healthy who need a doctor, but the sick.

Luke 5:30-31

The world screams. Politicians scream. Preachers even scream. Everyone is screaming, but God whispers "I love you" with every gentle breeze.

¹⁵so that you may become blameless and pure, children of God without fault in a crooked and depraved generation, in which you shine like stars in the universe.

Philippians 2:15

Do you have a mint condition faith? You weren't made to sit in a box on a shelf. God wants you to be used, tattered, & maybe even broken.

¹⁷The sacrifices of God are a broken spirit; a broken and contrite heart, O God, you will not despise.

Psalm 51:17

sep 11

Fear is a trap for the loveless. If you fear a certain element of society, try loving them and see what happens. Love drives out fear.

[18]There is no fear in love. But perfect love drives out fear, because fear has to do with punishment. The one who fears is not made perfect in love.

1 John 4:18

sep 12

Maturity is birthed through adversity. Pity the person who has faced no trials for they have missed the joy of faith in action.

[4]Perseverance must finish its work so that you may be mature and complete, not lacking anything.

James 1:4

sep 13

Christians are the salt of the earth. We add flavor to the world & are preservative agents to keep people from rotting on the inside.

13"You are the salt of the earth. But if the salt loses its saltiness, how can it be made salty again? It is no longer good for anything, except to be thrown out and trampled by men.

Matthew 5:13

sep 14

Just as consumerism propels & dictates every other facet of our lives it can replace Christ as your driving force. Guard your heart.

23Above all else, guard your heart, for it is the wellspring of life.

Proverbs 4:23

sep 15

When the hard truths of Jesus are unprotected they get replaced with fluffy notions that become the root of deep heresy & false doctrine.

³If anyone teaches false doctrines and does not agree to the sound instruction of our Lord Jesus Christ and to godly teaching, ⁴he is conceited and understands nothing. He has an unhealthy interest in controversies and quarrels about words that result in envy, strife, malicious talk, evil suspicions ⁵and constant friction between men of corrupt mind, who have been robbed of the truth and who think that godliness is a means to financial gain.

1 Timothy 6:3-5

sep 16

Uniting yourself to a local body of believers enables you to find true fellowship, authentic accountability, & sustained biblical teaching.

²My purpose is that they may be encouraged in heart and united in love, so that they may have the full riches of complete understanding, in order that they may know the mystery of God, namely, Christ, ³in whom are hidden all the treasures of wisdom and knowledge.

Colossians 2:2-3

sep 17

The Church is not a building, a set of programs, or a pastoral staff. People make up the Body of Christ. You are the Church.

⁹But you are a chosen people, a royal priesthood, a holy nation, a people belonging to God, that you may declare the praises of him who called you out of darkness into his wonderful light.

1 Peter 2:9

sep 18

Jesus is the LIFE. Everything you do apart from Him is a decaying mass of death, but all that you do with Him lasts forever.

⁶Jesus answered, "I am the way and the truth and the life. No one comes to the Father except through me.

John 14:6

sep 19

Jesus is the TRUTH. The truth is a person to be known, not a concept to be proven. You know the truth & can introduce truth to others.

²¹I do not write to you because you do not know the truth, but because you do know it and because no lie comes from the truth.

1 John 2:21

sep 20

Jesus is the WAY. The only way to get to where God wants you to be is to follow Jesus. Keep in step with the Spirit so that you do not lose your way.

¹"Do not let your hearts be troubled. Trust in God; trust also in me. ²In my Father's house are many rooms; if it were not so, I would have told you. I am going there to prepare a place for you. ³And if I go and prepare a place for you, I will come back and take you to be with me that you also may be where I am. ⁴You know the way to the place where I am going."

John 14:1-4

sep 21

Gathering clouds signal the coming storm as the sojourner's heart pounds. The waves grow fierce, but steady is the ship captained by Jesus.

²³Then he got into the boat and his disciples followed him. ²⁴Without warning, a furious storm came up on the lake, so that the waves swept over the boat. But Jesus was sleeping. ²⁵The disciples went and woke him, saying, "Lord, save us! We're going to drown!" ²⁶He replied, "You of little faith, why are you so afraid?" Then he got up and rebuked the winds and the waves, and it was completely calm. ²⁷The men were amazed and asked, "What kind of man is this? Even the winds and the waves obey him!"

Matthew 8:23-27

sep 22

Stagnant feet plod a course of destruction, while the swift of foot generate life with every eager step. Make the gospel be each day's destination.

¹⁵And how can they preach unless they are sent? As it is written, "How beautiful are the feet of those who bring good news!"

Romans 10:15

Our world is a lost & found box. People exist void of purpose waiting to be found & given function. The lost are here but is anyone looking?

²¹Jesus looked at him and loved him. "One thing you lack," he said. "Go, sell everything you have and give to the poor, and you will have treasure in heaven. Then come, follow me."

Mark 10:21

False doctrine is like candy for the soul. It tastes sweet & gives a jolt of energy, but ultimately leaves you fat & lethargic.

¹⁹Their destiny is destruction, their god is their stomach, and their glory is in their shame. Their mind is on earthly things.

Philippians 3:19

sep 25

What the world deems as trash, Jesus longs to redeem. Dive into the world's dumpster & reclaim the rejected.

¹⁴who gave himself for us to redeem us from all wickedness and to purify for himself a people that are his very own, eager to do what is good.

Titus 2:14

sep 26

The name of Jesus is like honey. It's sweet on the lips, sticks to the soul, & makes everything better. Sweeten the world by sharing Jesus.

²⁴Pleasant words are a honeycomb, sweet to the soul and healing to the bones.

Proverbs 16:24

sep 27

God's splendor surrounds us. His majesty often takes our breath away & leaves us to take steady pause as time stands still.

²Ascribe to the LORD the glory due his name; worship the LORD in the splendor of his holiness.

Psalm 29:2

sep 28

Majestic moments must be proclaimed. They demand to be shared. We relive them in others as we pass the experience on.

²⁸We proclaim him, admonishing and teaching everyone with all wisdom, so that we may present everyone perfect in Christ. ²⁹To this end I labor, struggling with all his energy, which so powerfully works in me.

Colossians 1:28-29

sep 29

The true joy of receiving Christ Jesus as lord and savior is never fully complete until we pass the experience on to others.

³We proclaim to you what we have seen and heard, so that you also may have fellowship with us. And our fellowship is with the Father and with his Son, Jesus Christ. ⁴We write this to make our joy complete.

1 John 1:3-4

sep 30

Who wears a tux & then puts on a dirty old sweat suit on top of it? You have been clothed with Christ. Don't cover Him with sin.

²⁶You are all sons of God through faith in Christ Jesus, ²⁷for all of you who were baptized into Christ have clothed yourselves with Christ.

Galatians 3:26-27

167

october

oct 1

If our identity is that we are light, then darkness has no power over us unless we choose to allow it. Darkness cannot overcome light.

⁵This is the message we have heard from him and declare to you: God is light; in him there is no darkness at all.

1 John 1:5

oct 2

If walking as Jesus walked was easy & full of material comforts everyone would do it. The truth is that it is a dangerous journey.

⁶Whoever claims to live in him must walk as Jesus did.

1 John 2:6

All living things grow. Trees grow. Grass grows. People grow. If we are alive in Christ, we must also grow.

10And we pray this in order that you may live a life worthy of the Lord and may please him in every way: bearing fruit in every good work, growing in the knowledge of God.

Colossians 1:10

It is a lie to think that we can arrive at a comfortable state of spirituality, secure in salvation but where Jesus is not too intrusive.

15If you love me, you will obey what I command.

John 14:15

oct 5

The commands of scripture are progressive in nature, always leading to a deeper knowledge & understanding of Jesus.

⁵For this very reason, make every effort to add to your faith goodness; and to goodness, knowledge; ⁶and to knowledge, self-control; and to self-control, perseverance; and to perseverance, godliness; ⁷and to godliness, brotherly kindness; and to brotherly kindness, love.

2 Peter 1:5-7

oct 6

Most people extend love like it is a limited resource. Love is limitless. God lavishes His love on us, so we can give out of abundance.

¹How great is the love the Father has lavished on us, that we should be called children of God! And that is what we are! The reason the world does not know us is that it did not know him.

1 John 3:1

oct 7

It is ludicrous to think that we have a God given right to be spared from pain, because we obey God. Suffering is a privilege for the godly.

²¹They preached the good news in that city and won a large number of disciples. Then they returned to Lystra, Iconium and Antioch, ²²strengthening the disciples and encouraging them to remain true to the faith. "We must go through many hardships to enter the kingdom of God," they said.

Acts 14:21-22

oct 8

Jesus is the standard against which all things are measured. Commit yourself to knowing Him & you will be able to test everything.

²¹Test everything. Hold on to the good.

1 Thessalonians 5:21

oct 9

The search for significance never turns out the way we plan. If Jesus dying for you doesn't make you feel significant, nothing will.

¹⁶For God so loved the world that he gave his one and only Son, that whoever believes in him shall not perish but have eternal life.

John 3:16

oct 10

The accumulation of more never satisfies. Keeping up with the Joneses can keep you from keeping up with Jesus.

²But as for me, my feet had almost slipped; I had nearly lost my foothold. ³For I envied the arrogant when I saw the prosperity of the wicked.

Psalm 73:2-3

oct 11

Perseverance rarely if ever disappoints, but quitters are haunted by the nagging "what ifs". Stand firm & know peace.

[11]As you know, we consider blessed those who have persevered. You have heard of Job's perseverance and have seen what the Lord finally brought about. The Lord is full of compassion and mercy.

James 5:11

oct 12

If only one thing could be said to describe your life, let it be said that you spent your years on earth loving deeply.

[11]Dear friends, since God so loved us, we also ought to love one another.

1 John 4:11

oct 13

Fortunes will be spent, buildings will crumble, and words will be forgotten. But love never fails. Love leaves no regrets.

⁹For we know in part and we prophesy in part.

1 Corinthians 13:9

oct 14

Love is our fuel. When we fail to submit ourselves to the love of God, we end up empty & motionless.

¹⁷so that Christ may dwell in your hearts through faith. And I pray that you, being rooted and established in love, ¹⁸may have power, together with all the saints, to grasp how wide and long and high and deep is the love of Christ, ¹⁹and to know this love that surpasses knowledge—that you may be filled to the measure of all the fullness of God.

Ephesians 3:17-19

oct 15

People tend to idealize & even encourage a little healthy rebellion, but every rebellious act against God is a direct offense to the cross.

³This is love for God: to obey his commands. And his commands are not burdensome, ⁴for everyone born of God overcomes the world. This is the victory that has overcome the world, even our faith. ⁵Who is it that overcomes the world? Only he who believes that Jesus is the Son of God.

1 John 5:3-5

oct 16

Fearing accountability prevents godly relationships. We hold nobody accountable, because we are terrified that they might return the favor.

¹⁵These, then, are the things you should teach. Encourage and rebuke with all authority. Do not let anyone despise you.

Titus 2:15

oct 17

The hyper-scheduled, over-sized, fast-paced rigmarole that we pursue in the name of abundant life leads to nowhere. Slow down.

²By the seventh day God had finished the work he had been doing; so on the seventh day he rested from all his work. ³And God blessed the seventh day and made it holy, because on it he rested from all the work of creating that he had done.

Genesis 2:2-3

oct 18

Freedom is best realized in love. When you put the needs of another first in love, you are free of the great bondage of selfishness.

³⁶Turn my heart toward your statutes and not toward selfish gain.

Psalm 119:36

179

A phantom lurks beneath the smug & confident demeanor of the self-righteous. The monster of self destroys all who don't depend on Jesus.

²¹But now a righteousness from God, apart from law, has been made known, to which the Law and the Prophets testify. ²²This righteousness from God comes through faith in Jesus Christ to all who believe.

Romans 3:21-22a

oct 20

Never exchange the grace of God for a spiritual checklist of "do's" & "don'ts". Grace will never disappoint, but law will always frustrate.

²¹I do not set aside the grace of God, for if righteousness could be gained through the law, Christ died for nothing!"

Galatians 2:21

oct 21

The circular logic that drives the expulsion of God from scientific reason will ultimately leave a dizzy & bewildered mass of humanity.

¹The fool says in his heart, "There is no God."

Psalm 14:1a

---

oct 22

The next time someone tells you that there is no such thing as "absolute truth" respond by asking them if they are absolutely sure.

⁵Into your hands I commit my spirit; redeem me, O LORD, the God of truth.

Psalm 31:5

181

oct 23

Christians must be willing to think & be questioned. We have power through Jesus to demolish every argument that opposes God.

³For though we live in the world, we do not wage war as the world does. ⁴The weapons we fight with are not the weapons of the world. On the contrary, they have divine power to demolish strongholds.

2 Corinthians 10:3-4

oct 24

No task is ever beneath a truly righteous person. Righteousness removes any notion of pride that would hinder genuine servant hood.

²⁸just as the Son of Man did not come to be served, but to serve, and to give his life as a ransom for many."

Matthew 20:28

oct 25

Take care of your body. Physical discipline will only enhance your spiritual discipline. Practice a holistic relationship with Jesus.

[13]Do not offer the parts of your body to sin, as instruments of wickedness, but rather offer yourselves to God, as those who have been brought from death to life; and offer the parts of your body to him as instruments of righteousness.

Romans 6:13

oct 26

Creation screams "there is a God". How dull are the senses that are capable of tuning that out? God is our most obvious reality.

[20]For since the creation of the world God's invisible qualities—his eternal power and divine nature—have been clearly seen, being understood from what has been made, so that men are without excuse.

Romans 1:20

oct 27

Live to please Jesus. Living to please self or others denies you the ability to follow Jesus. You can only have one master.

¹⁰Am I now trying to win the approval of men, or of God? Or am I trying to please men? If I were still trying to please men, I would not be a servant of Christ.

Galatians 1:10

oct 28

Faith is put to the test when God asks you to do something that is counter-intuitive. Faith is trusting God even when it makes no sense.

¹⁷By faith Abraham, when God tested him, offered Isaac as a sacrifice. He who had received the promises was about to sacrifice his one and only son, ¹⁸even though God had said to him, "It is through Isaac that your offspring will be reckoned."

Hebrews 11:17-18

oct 29

Jesus has called you out & delivered you from death. You are free to go wherever you want except back into the tomb of sin & death.

⁴³When he had said this, Jesus called in a loud voice, "Lazarus, come out!" ⁴⁴The dead man came out, his hands and feet wrapped with strips of linen, and a cloth around his face. Jesus said to them, "Take off the grave clothes and let him go."

John 11:43-44

oct 30

An act of kindness can sometimes get you into trouble. When was the last time you got in trouble for Jesus?

⁸Then Peter, filled with the Holy Spirit, said to them: "Rulers and elders of the people! ⁹If we are being called to account today for an act of kindness shown to a cripple and are asked how he was healed, ¹⁰then know this, you and all the people of Israel: It is by the name of Jesus Christ of Nazareth, whom you crucified but whom God raised from the dead, that this man stands before you healed.

Acts 4:8-10

185

oct 31

The temptation to don a mask is an everyday affair. Most live as though they are playing a part on the world's stage. Simply be yourself.

²⁴A malicious man disguises himself with his lips, but in his heart he harbors deceit.

Proverbs 26:24

november

The physical laws of nature are no match for our God. Whatever your dilemma, you can rest assured that God is capable of delivering you.

¹³Moses answered the people, "Do not be afraid. Stand firm and you will see the deliverance the LORD will bring you today. The Egyptians you see today you will never see again. ¹⁴The LORD will fight for you; you need only to be still."

Exodus 14:13-14

Do people praise God because of you? Live in such a way that people who encounter you are driven to worship God.

²⁴And they praised God because of me.

Galatians 1:24

nov 3

> Once upon a time, God spoke & it was. God promised & it happened. God died & came back to life. All good news, but the best is yet to come.

¹In the beginning was the Word, and the Word was with God, and the Word was God. ²He was with God in the beginning. ³Through him all things were made; without him nothing was made that has been made. ⁴In him was life, and that life was the light of men. hese, then, are the things you should teach. Encourage and rebuke with all authority. Do not let anyone despise you.

John 1:1-4

nov 4

> For the Christian, everything is spiritual. Everything is Christ. Nothing is irrelevant. Every moment of every day is His & is meaningful.

²⁰I have been crucified with Christ and I no longer live, but Christ lives in me. The life I live in the body, I live by faith in the Son of God, who loved me and gave himself for me.

Galatians 2:20

> If we call ourselves Christians & do nothing to eradicate darkness, we are revealed as liars. We are light. Darkness doesn't stand a chance.

8For you were once darkness, but now you are light in the Lord. Live as children of light.

Ephesians 5:8

> God designs, calls, & equips us to serve. Serving is simply submitting to the will of God. How can that ever burn us out?

29To this end I labor, struggling with all his energy, which so powerfully works in me.

Colossians 1:29

When we only see what we want to see & ignore the things that God is drawing us to see, we live in the darkness of self-deception.

²²The eye is the lamp of the body. If your eyes are good, your whole body will be full of light. ²³But if your eyes are bad, your whole body will be full of darkness. If then the light within you is darkness, how great is that darkness!

Matthew 6:22-23

Keeping in step with the Holy Spirit leaves no time for sin. Following Jesus is a full-time deal. Pause for sin & you fall out of step.

¹⁶So I say, live by the Spirit, and you will not gratify the desires of the sinful nature.

Galatians 5:16

nov 9

There is no such thing as partial surrender. Following Jesus is an all-or-nothing proposition.

²¹Jesus answered, "If you want to be perfect, go, sell your possessions and give to the poor, and you will have treasure in heaven. Then come, follow me." ²²When the young man heard this, he went away sad, because he had great wealth.

Matthew 19:21-22

nov 10

A conceited Christian has lost their way. Any notion of "I'm better than you" can't come from God. Remember who you were apart from Christ.

²⁶Let us not become conceited, provoking and envying each other.

Galatians 5:26

nov 11

> Sin confrontation should be done for the purpose of restoration. It is not about punishment & should be done gently & lovingly.

[1]Brothers, if someone is caught in a sin, you who are spiritual should restore him gently. But watch yourself, or you also may be tempted.

Galatians 6:1

---

nov 12

> The smallest imperfection makes the greatest perfection completely imperfect. Perfection is the standard. Nothing short of that measures up.

[11]Finally, brothers, good-by. Aim for perfection, listen to my appeal, be of one mind, live in peace. And the God of love and peace will be with you.

2 Corinthians 13:11

nov 13

God's challenge isn't just to lead a good life, to be a decent person, or to be better than the average guy. Jesus' challenge is perfection.

⁴⁸Be perfect, therefore, as your heavenly Father is perfect.

Matthew 5:48

nov 14

Boast about Jesus. Talk about the great things He has done so much that everyone knows without a doubt that He is your greatest love.

¹⁴May I never boast except in the cross of our Lord Jesus Christ, through which the world has been crucified to me, and I to the world.

Galatians 6:14

195

nov 15

God's blessing has been given to you through Jesus. If you find that blessing to be insufficient you do not grasp the reality of it.

³Praise be to the God and Father of our Lord Jesus Christ, who has blessed us in the heavenly realms with every spiritual blessing in Christ.

Ephesians 1:3

nov 16

The love of God is the driving force of the universe as God is defined by love. Love permeates and propels His every action.

⁸Whoever does not love does not know God, because God is love.

1 John 4:8

nov 17

Recognizing the depth of our own depravity is a catalyst for extravagant worship. Whoever has been forgiven much will love much.

⁴⁷Therefore, I tell you, her many sins have been forgiven—for she loved much. But he who has been forgiven little loves little."

Luke 7:47

nov 18

Be bold in prayer. Ask for the extraordinary. Seek the divine. Confidently make your appeal & ask God to do more than you are capable of.

¹²In him and through faith in him we may approach God with freedom and confidence.

Ephesians 3:12

197

> The breakfast of champions is the Word of God. Devour His Word & it will sustain you through every trail & temptation each day brings.

¹Then Jesus was led by the Spirit into the desert to be tempted by the devil. ²After fasting forty days and forty nights, he was hungry. ³The tempter came to him and said, "If you are the Son of God, tell these stones to become bread." ⁴Jesus answered, "It is written: 'Man does not live on bread alone, but on every word that comes from the mouth of God.'"

Matthew 4:1-4

> The toleration of personal sin creates a calloused heart. When sensitivity to the depravity of sin is lost, indulgence increases.

¹⁹Having lost all sensitivity, they have given themselves over to sensuality so as to indulge in every kind of impurity, with a continual lust for more.

Ephesians 4:19

nov 21

Make your life a slippery slope for the devil. Be so covered in holiness that there is nothing for him to grab onto.

27and do not give the devil a foothold.

Ephesians 4:27

nov 22

The pursuit of lifestyle maintenance instead of Kingdom expansion is one of the greatest and most ignored abuses of the cross.

29"I tell you the truth," Jesus replied, "no one who has left home or brothers or sisters or mother or father or children or fields for me and the gospel 30will fail to receive a hundred times as much in this present age (homes, brothers, sisters, mothers, children and fields—and with them, persecutions) and in the age to come, eternal life. 31But many who are first will be last, and the last first."

Mark 10:29-31

199

nov 23

Imitation is the greatest form of flattery. If you want to please God, simply imitate Him. Begin with laying down your life.

¹Be imitators of God, therefore, as dearly loved children ²and live a life of love, just as Christ loved us and gave himself up for us as a fragrant offering and sacrifice to God.

Ephesians 5:1-2

nov 24

Light exposes darkness. Darkness can never defeat light. The only way for darkness to exist in our world is if Christians refuse to shine.

⁸For you were once darkness, but now you are light in the Lord. Live as children of light ⁹(for the fruit of the light consists in all goodness, righteousness and truth) ¹⁰and find out what pleases the Lord.

Ephesians 5:8-10

nov 25

We never need to pray that God would be with us. He is always with us. The more appropriate pray is that we would be aware of His presence.

⁷Tremble, O earth, at the presence of the Lord, at the presence of the God of Jacob.

Psalm 114:7

nov 26

Take delight in the commands of God. He gives them to enhance your life not to diminish it. Abundant living begins with obedience.

¹Praise the LORD. Blessed is the man who fears the LORD, who finds great delight in his commands.

Psalm 112:1

Life with Jesus is fun. It is never boring. It is always an adventure. Each day presents fresh opportunities to participate in the divine.

14Satisfy us in the morning with your unfailing love, that we may sing for joy and be glad all our days.

Psalm 90:14

When you find yourself in over your head, at the end of your rope, & at rock bottom you are in the perfect position to be used by God.

27But God chose the foolish things of the world to shame the wise; God chose the weak things of the world to shame the strong.

1 Corinthians 1:27

nov 29

When all hope is lost, Jesus turns the tables & does the unthinkable. He rose from the dead. Surely He can handle your problems.

⁶"Don't be alarmed," he said. "You are looking for Jesus the Nazarene, who was crucified. He has risen! He is not here. See the place where they laid him.

Mark 16:6

nov 30

The fear of offending often halts the spread of the gospel. Be overzealous with the gospel & for the love of God offend somebody with it.

¹¹Never be lacking in zeal, but keep your spiritual fervor, serving the Lord.

Romans 12:11

december

dec 1

The greatest gift of Christmas is Immanuel, God is with us. If you are not dwelling in the fullness of Jesus, you haven't received the gift.

23"The virgin will be with child and will give birth to a son, and they will call him Immanuel"—which means, "God with us."

Matthew 1:23

dec 2

The craziest part of the holiday hustle & bustle is that in our dash to make the perfect preparations we often fail to prepare our hearts.

2Set your minds on things above, not on earthly things.

Colossians 3:2

dec 3

When God calls us He interrupts our plans and changes the course of our lives. It can be a troubling thing to be chosen by God.

²⁸The angel went to her and said, "Greetings, you who are highly favored! The Lord is with you." ²⁹Mary was greatly troubled at his words and wondered what kind of greeting this might be.

Luke 1:28-29

dec 4

Despite the enemy's greatest efforts, Christmas still comes back to one crucial event…the birth of Jesus.

⁶While they were there, the time came for the baby to be born, ⁷and she gave birth to her firstborn, a son. She wrapped him in cloths and placed him in a manger, because there was no room for them in the inn.

Luke 2:6-7

dec 5

Our perfect gift to God is a surrendered heart & an obedient life. Go ahead & splurge this Christmas & give yourself completely to God.

¹¹On coming to the house, they saw the child with his mother Mary, and they bowed down and worshiped him. Then they opened their treasures and presented him with gifts of gold and of incense and of myrrh.

Matthew 2:11

dec 6

The songs of Christmas are fantastic reminders of the greatest story ever told. Sing loudly & sing with joy!

¹⁹Speak to one another with psalms, hymns and spiritual songs. Sing and make music in your heart to the Lord, ²⁰always giving thanks to God the Father for everything, in the name of our Lord Jesus Christ.

Ephesians 5:19-20

dec 7

The anticipation of Christmas seen through the sparkling eyes of a child is exactly how we should anticipate His great & glorious return.

[12]"Behold, I am coming soon! My reward is with me, and I will give to everyone according to what he has done.

Revelation 22:12

dec 8

For many, Christmas is merely an excuse for indulging. Avoid gluttony & materialism this Christmas & indulge in worship instead.

[20]The shepherds returned, glorifying and praising God for all the things they had heard and seen, which were just as they had been told.

Luke 2:20

dec 9

Christmas is full of treasures under the tree waiting to be unwrapped, but may the greatest treasure of all remain securely in your heart.

¹⁹But Mary treasured up all these things and pondered them in her heart.

Luke 2:19

---

dec 10

Christmas is the perfect time to proclaim the amazingness of Jesus. Shout it out. Sing it out. Give it away!

¹⁷When they had seen him, they spread the word concerning what had been told them about this child.

Luke 2:17

dec 11

> The announcement of Christ's birth came with passion & power. We share in that power every time we announce Jesus to another.

⁸And there were shepherds living out in the fields nearby, keeping watch over their flocks at night. ⁹An angel of the Lord appeared to them, and the glory of the Lord shone around them, and they were terrified. ¹⁰But the angel said to them, "Do not be afraid. I bring you good news of great joy that will be for all the people.

Luke 2:8-10

dec 12

> The fact that there was no room in the inn for baby Jesus is sad, but it's far sadder that many still have no room for Him in their hearts.

⁷and she gave birth to her firstborn, a son. She wrapped him in cloths and placed him in a manger, because there was no room for them in the inn.

Luke 2:7

dec 13

The arrival of Jesus changes everything. Kings take notice & everyone is disturbed. Pray that Jesus will disturb your Christmas.

¹After Jesus was born in Bethlehem in Judea, during the time of King Herod, Magi from the east came to Jerusalem ²and asked, "Where is the one who has been born king of the Jews? We saw his star in the east and have come to worship him." ³When King Herod heard this he was disturbed, and all Jerusalem with him.

Matthew 2:1-3

---

dec 14

God chose an ordinary woman & an ordinary man to be His Son's parents, because He can. He can also choose you to do the extraordinary.

¹⁸This is how the birth of Jesus Christ came about: His mother Mary was pledged to be married to Joseph, but before they came together, she was found to be with child through the Holy Spirit.

Matthew 1:18

dec 15

Memories of Christmas past have the power to haunt or bless. Utilize selective memory & ponder the glory & wonder of what God has done.

²Great are the works of the LORD; they are pondered by all who delight in them.

Psalm 111:2

dec 16

The true Christmas present is His presence in every present moment. Pray that your Christmas present be filled with Jesus.

²⁰And surely I am with you always, to the very end of the age.

Matthew 28:20b

dec 17

The grandness of Christmas future is that every day is a celebration of Christ's arrival. He is with us each new day & every situation.

⁸Jesus Christ is the same yesterday and today and forever.

Hebrews 13:8

dec 18

If you are dreaming of a white Christmas, stop praying for snow & simply look within yourself. Jesus has washed you whiter than snow.

⁷Cleanse me with hyssop, and I will be clean; wash me, and I will be whiter than snow.

Psalm 51:7

dec 19

Lights on a tree brighten the Christmas celebration. The light of Jesus within your soul brightens every dark corner of the human condition.

¹⁴"You are the light of the world. A city on a hill cannot be hidden.

Matthew 5:14

dec 20

The Christmas star announced the arrival of Messiah. Does your life proclaim that Jesus has arrived?

¹²Live such good lives among the pagans that, though they accuse you of doing wrong, they may see your good deeds and glorify God on the day he visits us.

1 Peter 2:12

dec 21

Every Grinch will attempt to steal your Christmas joy. Guard your heart & remain joyful regardless of your circumstances.

¹⁶Be joyful always;

1 Thessalonians 5:16

dec 22

Ribbons, bows, & shinny paper cause the mind to wonder. God wrapped Himself in humanity. Unwrap the glory of Jesus & be filled with wonder.

¹⁴The Word became flesh and made his dwelling among us. We have seen his glory, the glory of the One and Only, who came from the Father, full of grace and truth.

John 1:14

dec 23

The perfect Christmas has nothing to do with your perfectly executed plans, but everything to do with God's perfectly executed plan.

40God had planned something better for us so that only together with us would they be made perfect.

Hebrews 11:40

dec 24

If you find yourself caught under the mistletoe, do not panic. Kissing is biblical. Be warm & hospitable welcoming others into your home.

12Greet one another with a holy kiss.

2 Corinthians 13:12

dec 25

Once upon a Christmas a baby was born that would change the world. This Christmas can be a time when Jesus changes everything for you.

⁶For to us a child is born, to us a son is given, and the government will be on his shoulders. And he will be called Wonderful Counselor, Mighty God, Everlasting Father, Prince of Peace.

Isaiah 9:6

Merry Christmas!

dec 26

It is difficult to wait for God & trust His timing. When we weary with waiting we take matters into our own hands & thwart God's agenda.

¹⁴Wait for the LORD; be strong and take heart and wait for the LORD.

Psalm 27:14

dec 27

The closest distance between 2 points is a straight line. If you want to be closer to God, avoid the crooked path & walk straight.

[5]Trust in the LORD with all your heart and lean not on your own understanding; [6]in all your ways acknowledge him, and he will make your paths straight.

Proverbs 3:5-6

dec 28

The repulsion many feel towards Christianity is the loss of personal identity. Unless you become like Christ you have no part in Him.

[66]From this time many of his disciples turned back and no longer followed him.

John 6:66

dec 29

Does your faith have power or is it wimpy? Holy Spirit driven faith will make you a world changer. Power will fill every step you take.

8But you will receive power when the Holy Spirit comes on you; and you will be my witnesses in Jerusalem, and in all Judea and Samaria, and to the ends of the earth."

Acts 1:8

dec 30

A quarrelsome Christian is a tool of the Devil. Civil wars in the church & home distract us from the real battle for the salvation of souls.

2Be completely humble and gentle; be patient, bearing with one another in love. 3Make every effort to keep the unity of the Spirit through the bond of peace.

Ephesians 4:2-3

dec 31

Reflect on all that God has done in & through you over the last 12 months. Rejoice in God's faithfulness & offer genuine thanksgiving.

⁵But I trust in your unfailing love; my heart rejoices in your salvation.

Psalm 13:5